ON BEING DRAWN

PETER COLE AND
TERRY WINTERS

On Being Drawn

*an ekphrastic translation
(with commentary)*

CENTER FOR WRITERS & TRANSLATORS
THE AMERICAN UNIVERSITY OF PARIS

—

SYLPH EDITIONS

Foreword

IN THE SPRING OF 2017 Terry Winters asked me to contribute poems to the catalogue for a show he was planning at the Drawing Center in New York. I'd been finding my way for several years into the folds of what I'd come to think of as deep translation, the movement not just from one language and culture to another but from one medium to another, and throughout that exploration I was struck by the fact that the process of composing poems in response to works of art felt uncannily – and happily – like being inside the process of literary translation.

With the muscle memory of that sensation fresh, and turning to Terry's drawings, I wanted to see what would happen if I consciously approached the writing as I would a translation. That is, I took seriously a figure that's often used casually – of 'translating experience' from one part of life (or the brain) to another, which in this case entailed rendering my experience of the drawings into poems. In short, ekphrasis as translation. But also, it seemed to me – after I'd written the poems, and thought back to where this experiment began – translation as ekphrasis.

The cahier explores the dynamics of what I'll call embodied ekphrasis, a reimagining that doesn't simply present a description or illustrative interpretation of another artwork – a 'speaking out of', as the etymology of 'ekphrasis' has it – so much as it offers an account of being inside the work, of having it in oneself. This is what I believe good translation does, and why the absorption of a given 'original', before a translated word gets written down, is, as I hear it, the heart of the whole affair. As the rest is a matter of limbs and nerves. Or nerve.

Also part of the sympathetic identification driving this project is my longer-term involvement with Terry's art. And here I'm using 'sympathy' not only, or even primarily, in the emotional sense, to highlight 'feeling', but as it's employed in physics, where it indicates a relation between bodies in which vibrations in one cause the same in another. ('I guess the important thing is to copy down whatever vibration you see while your attention is strong', notes a noted oracle.) I knew and felt close to Terry's work, and *he* had extended the invitation to *me*. There was trust, but also a certain risk. What if I didn't like the drawings in this exhibition?

What if he didn't like what I wrote? This too is very much part of the translational dynamic at the core of even the most basic human interactions, with others and also ourselves.

The twelve drawings I 'translated' into 'original poems' were selected from the eighty or so included in the show that opened in April 2018. They cover the full range of Terry's career, though in choosing these particular drawings I was in no way trying to be representative; I was simply doing what I've done with the literary translations that have mattered most to me – following out a line of affinity.

The prose that's woven in grey throughout was written a good deal later, and acts as a kind of voice-under. It's meant to serve as commentary to the whole – to the specific poems and how they translate the art, and to the broader poetics of relation that, when all goes well (and sometimes when it doesn't), brings just about everything, it seems, into magnetic tension.

P.C.

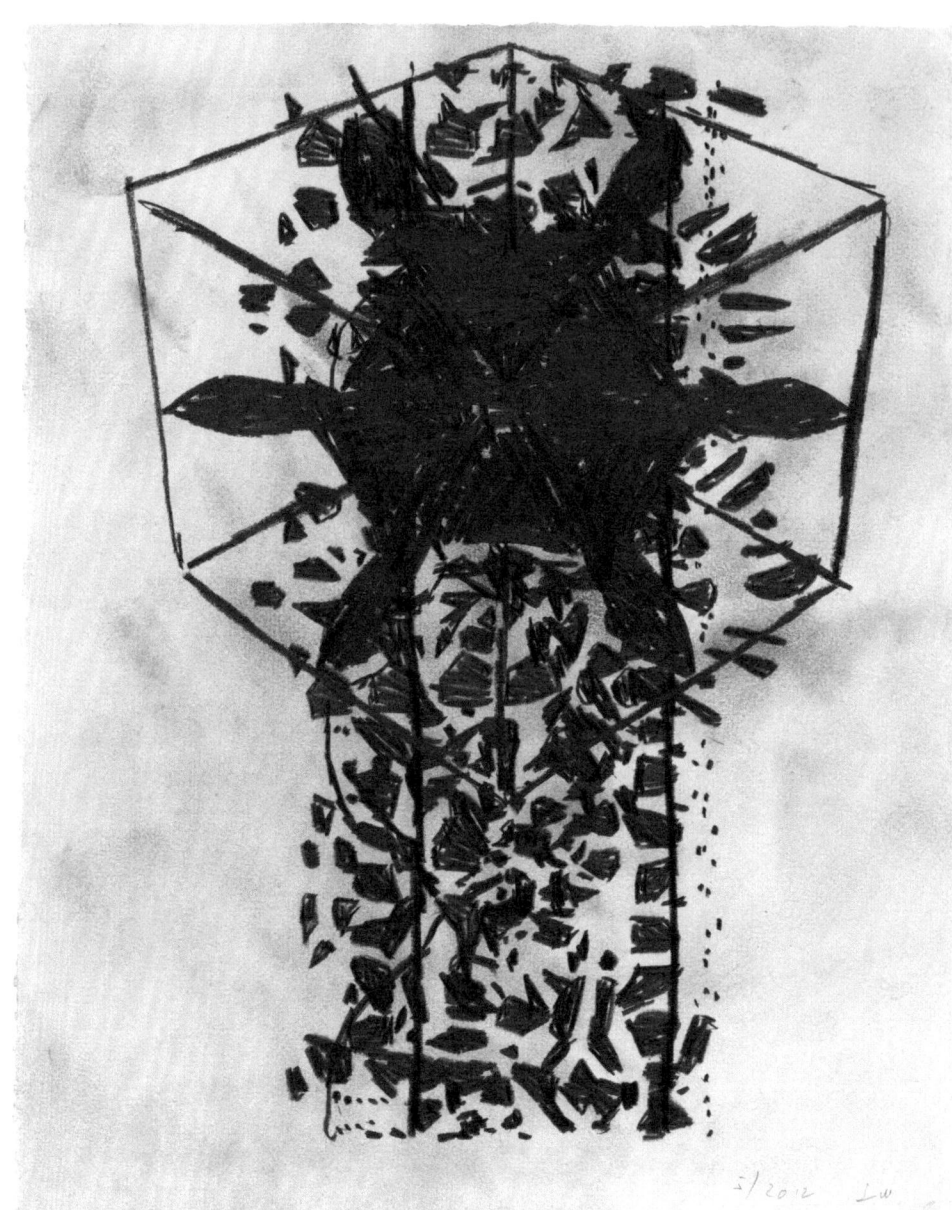

I

Drawing draws us in-
volving us further and stretching
attention it sketches reaching
inching in ink and grasping
graphite graphing drawing
draws us out of our cells
and selves extending thinking
into seeing what was
sensed or seen as something
once in hand an eye
or at the fingers' tips
it leads one on to a place
of twos and too and into
depths and arcs as angles
curve through layered swerves
and lines as tines drawing
is first and quickest to
the quick and draw and yet it
slows and flows unfolding
time raveling mine it
tries out signs along
a way a wavering it's
a doodle dancing within
its perfect incompletion
now a mesh and not a
mess a net at work
along a seam between us
drawing seems to hone
what might be true and turn
by turn it trains but doesn't
tame. Like runes. It tunes us.

II

>Charcoal's quiet and chalky mist
>seed a cone's emergence from its
>sinking here now into the page
>as   and of its absence and grays
>there and not quite there yet mix.

There's nothing to explain. Its silence says it all. And yet – the drawing calls. And continues to draw. Like every original, it's born in translation of a sort, which is to say, a carrying across, from one plane of discovery to another. And that conveyance encodes the calling, to which the poem responds – a kind of looking rendered as a rhythm, a sound extension in time; a trafficking (or trade) between, as the root of *interpret* suggests. The texture and tension of the verse, the distribution of weights and density along the lines and down them emerged, or so it seemed in the process of composition, physically from what drew me in. That subtle shifting from nothing to something and then to something more and back to nothing again, at its margin or heart, was what (in a nutshell?) I wanted the poem to capture and release:

That these nuts to crack hold seeds, and are at once themselves and strange, and at a stage, or on one. They mirror what we know, and more. Or more so. They hover. Nothing is happening, within the frame. No one is speaking or thinking through them. And then we are – in the drawing, and moved, across a gap between, finding ourselves beyond ourselves, translated into a tiny but borderless kingdom of scumbling and shades, marks and matte (or lambent) greys, at hand, and drifting through us. Making our day, in their curious ways.

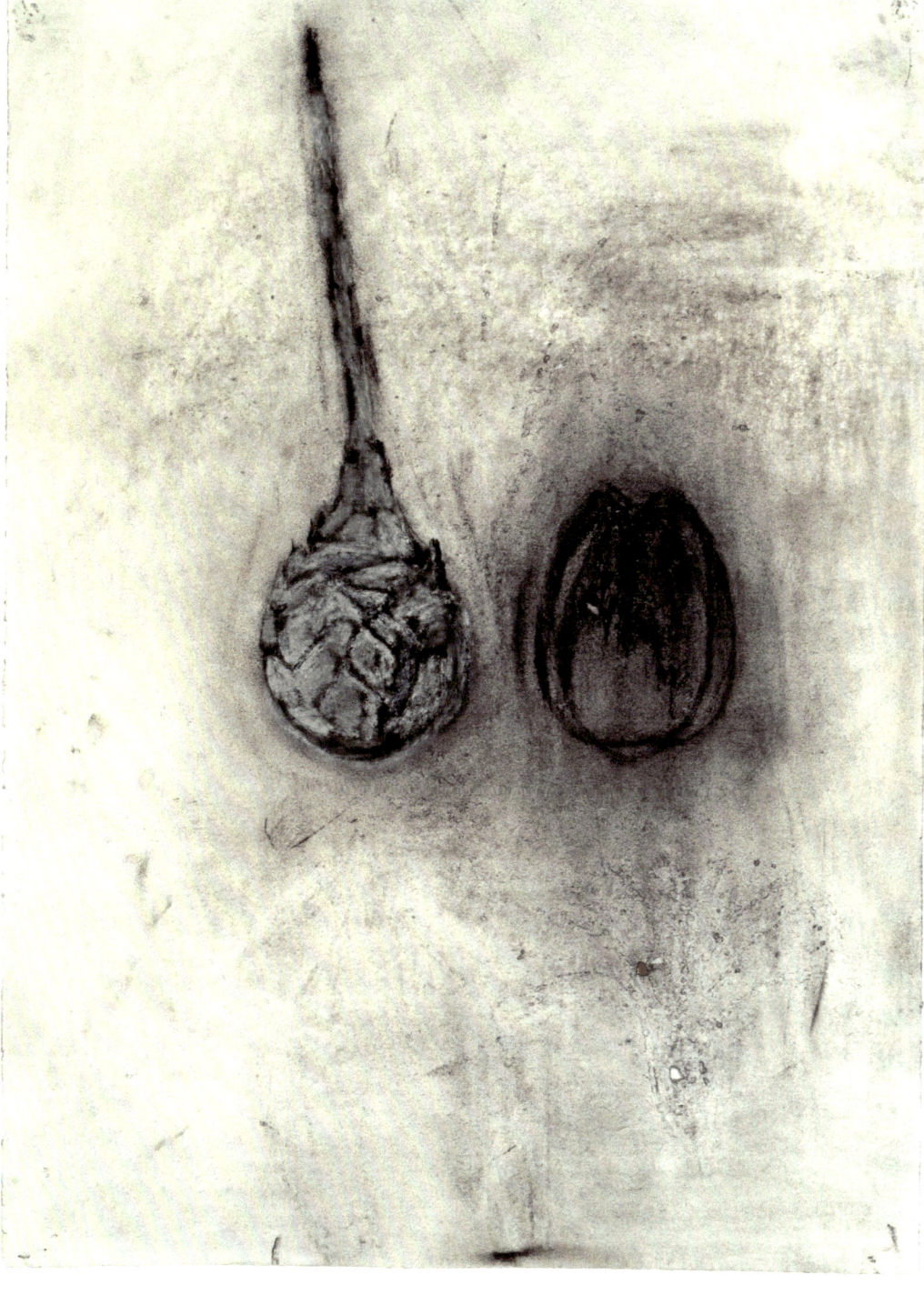

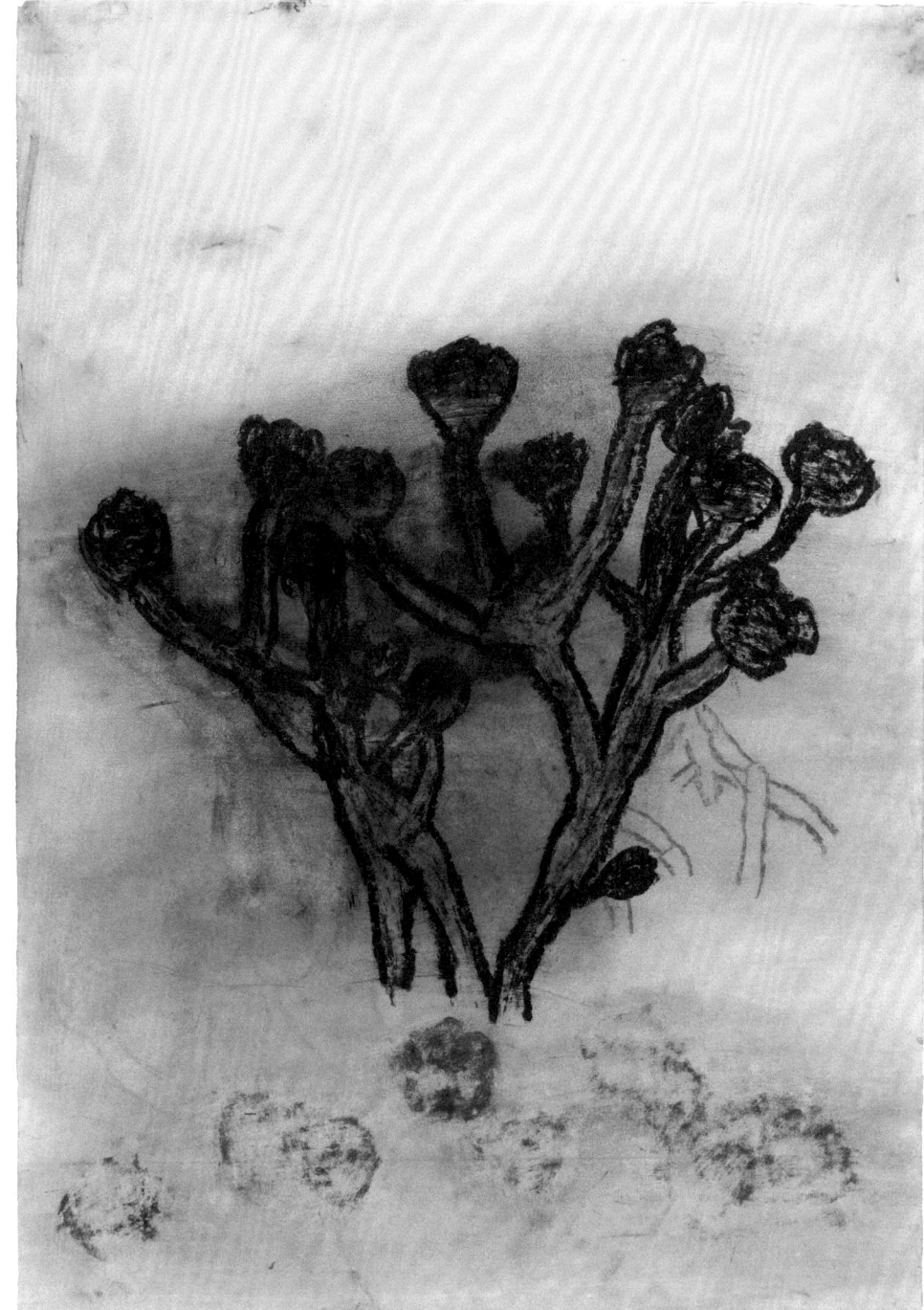

Draw me after you, let us run, says the Song, of all Songs (1:4) –
which the Spanish kabbalists gloss, in their *Book of Radiance*:
'Each letter called to the others.'

And then: *The King has brought me into his chambers*, construed
by that *Radiance* as – into the midst of the letters and their spell,
an Eden of understanding, lurking in what we think and dream,
write and say.

'All those drawings of the Dwelling' . . . 'all the worlds above
depending below upon the letters' mystery'.

And this is the Eros of our listening –

which yields, in its slightly preposterous way, the prosody these
poems aim to embody, in their dwelling on the drawing. An
almost homophonic response – to that mute (yet musical) original,
as though at Sinai, in Exodus 20, after Scripture has been revealed,
all the people saw the sounds (*kolot*). So in these poems I was writing
to *hear the drawing*.

―――

> This dark plant glows with its ground
> and grows from a black fire of whiteness –
> so boundlessness pulses, nearly in hand.
> Its smudged halo holds, like a kiss,
> creation's lipstick, a fooling around.

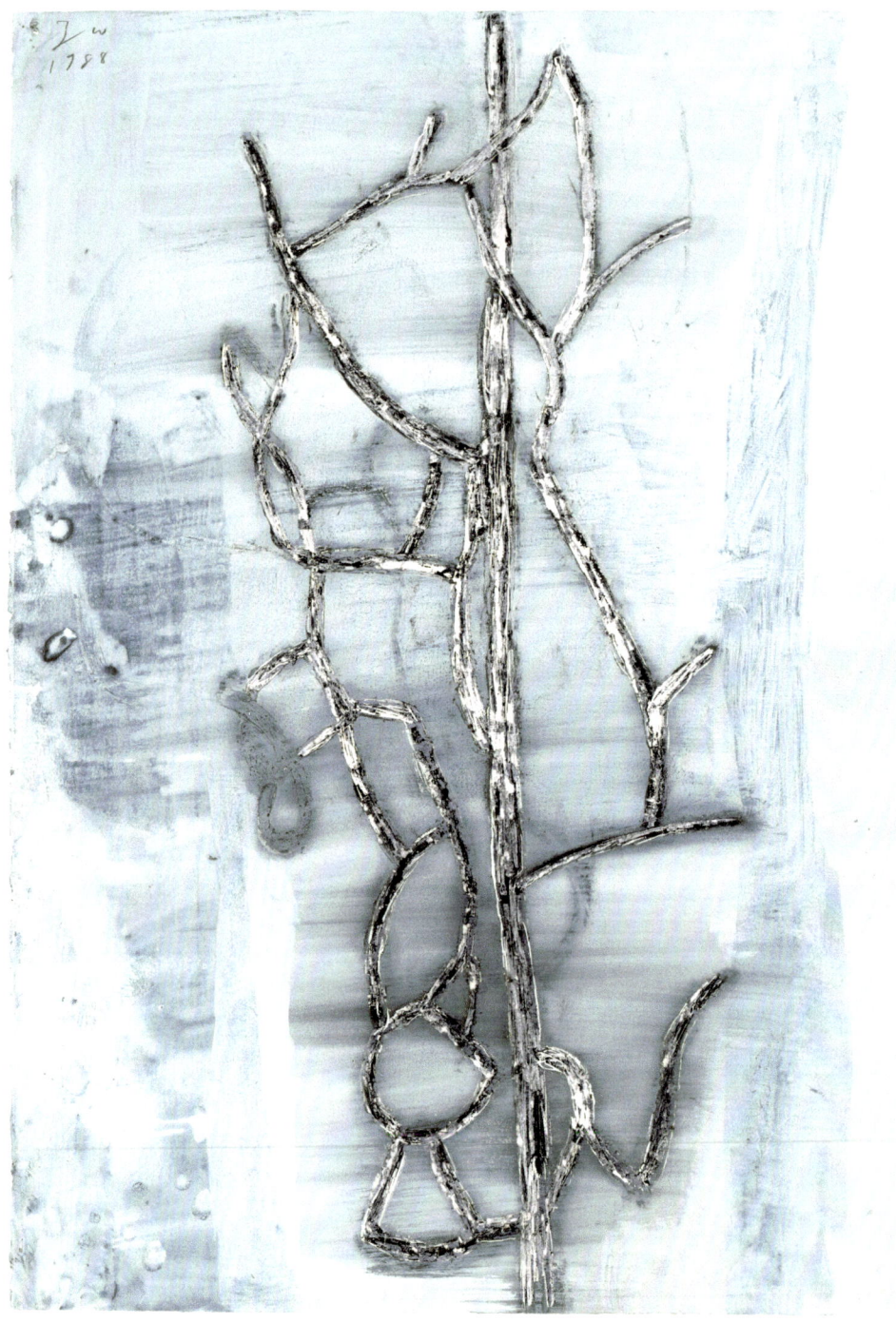

> The nerve and zinc ascent of it:
> descending extension in every direction –
> knots of cinder and brightness as one
> wash of ash through which it hums
> beneath the skin   these paths are thought.

———

The smudged sounds give rise to lines, a syntax like synapses. Grappa in its capillary action. The narrow descent paradoxically widens out and lifts along a spectrum of endless adjacencies, 'in every direction, and every inflection,' as Levi Yitzhak of Berditchev sang, in his gentle Yiddish, 'Still You. However You. Only You. Ever You…'

    You, the viewer? The reader? Whoever you are, and where… Drawing really does – draw us in (to the object rendered and the time taken) and out (of ourselves to further seeing and other surfaces, even souls, or simply tensility sensed).

'My small skill to save a likeness,' John Berger writes of his own sketching his father's final face in its coffin.

But in the case of these almost abstract sketches, a likeness of what? And how might that 'what' be tricked into speech?

It isn't always pleasant. The act itself and the realization – that part of a translation's depth derives from its movement through death. The total identification with an original leading to its replacement, so that another's name and lines live on. So the present unfurls as a rickety bridge of resemblances, and resurrections. And the translator, too, passes away again and again through self-effacement faced. For now. And after? An afterlife, after all?

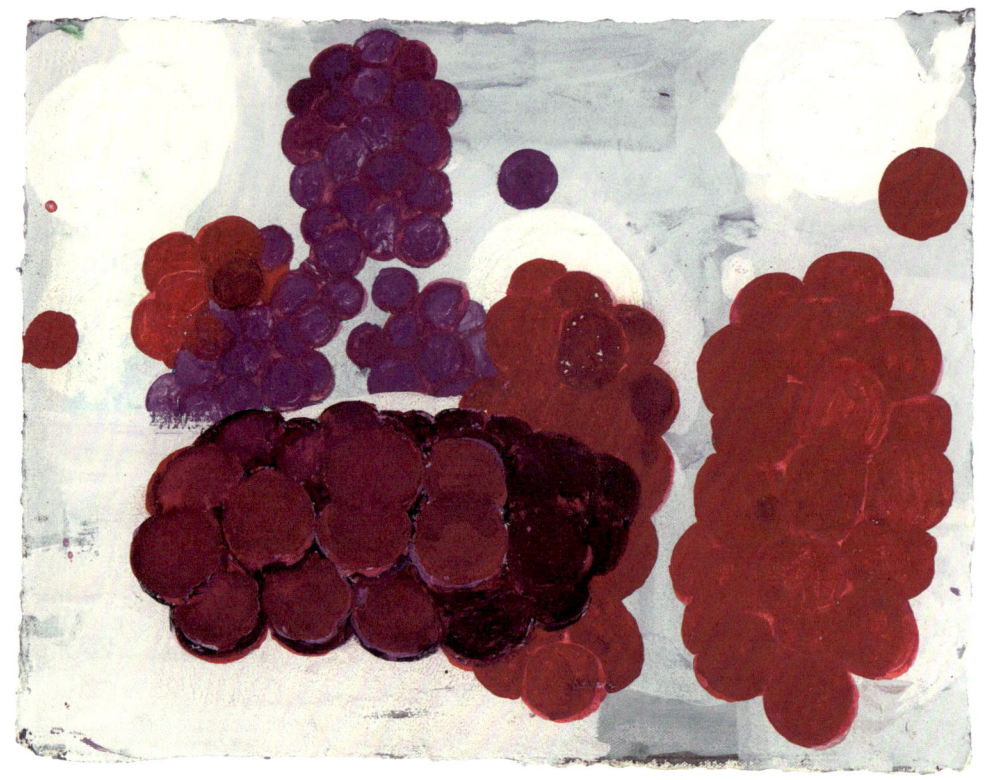

III

Odd how globs form morulae
or constellations of single cells
evolve as clocks of grape-like clouds
and scarlet clusters hovering near
smears of a maculate whiteness become
the drifting stalk and jot of an 'i'…

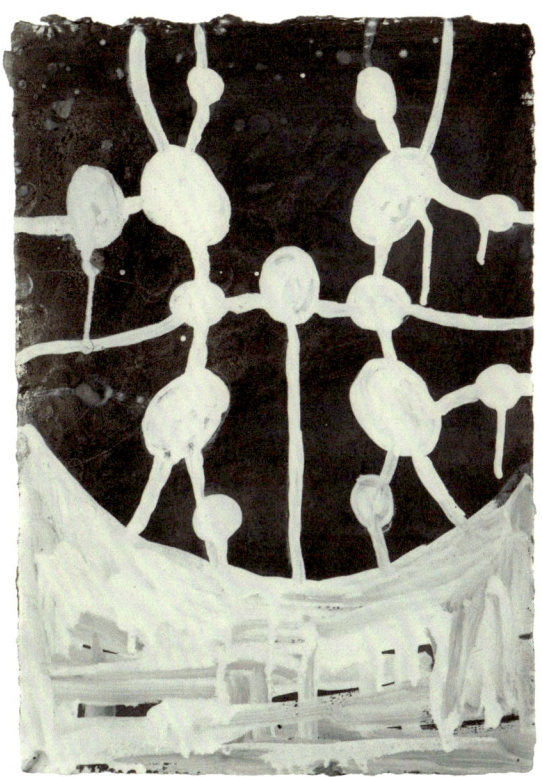

*

Neurons fire
in black and white
(gouache and graphite)
and unlike angels
don't expire
with ignition
along a spine
reaching the head
we wander into
the frame and opening
of an interim
installation
to which all roads
have suddenly led

Contamination's centripetal, at first, a listening into skin.

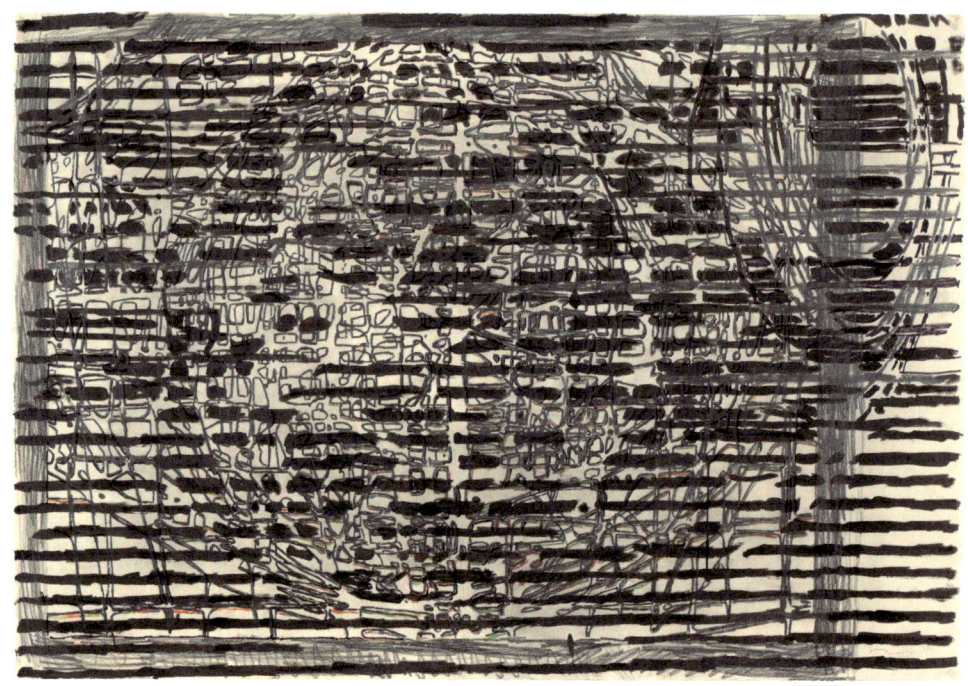

⋆

The eye slides beyond the rendering's
frame and out through just about
everything now we're seeing there
in these blinding lines, elided…

Wisdom burrows in the art of drawing, and the drawing becomes
a kind of proverb, also for one's dwelling – as in the *templum*
of contemplation, where birds in flight and viscera were read.
And this too shifts through verse, down and dirty in its purity,
like a body.

I.e., *there but for the grace of clouds go eyes that reach and lead at once
a lease and leash on life and sighs*
 – rides the sensory cusp of
nonsense, the voids that open up in speech, and what it's
depicting. And yet, the sentence is like a sill before a view I heard;
it speaks to something there I knew and

No, I never really let's say rarely really see without a feeling that
I'm missing something, who isn't? Just to look's a lucking out a
window's pane or maybe into a framing –

on which so much depends: where you put the frame and how.
Seeing is what we've been taught to allow, and follow through...

A meeting (of minds, yes, but more so) of mediums.

Rhyme's a rhizome,   In media theory
rhyme is loam.   in medias res
When it's foam   in theory beyond
the poem's not done.   an outlier's guess
The poem's not done   Non-hierarchical
until it's a dome   arches depend
(the dome itself   and quasi-farsical –
is a kind of poem)   your life's in your hands
and even then   Always off-center
there's more to come,   and multiplicitous
as the rhizome roams   slantwise rooting
and its phonemes run   like an iris
up and slantwise   its iodine flame
down at once,   for a moment extends
through its phloem –   fringed with beards
the poem is one.   as signs of &s
Through its phloem.   as its ex-
The poem is done.   hibition ends

———

Are poems translations of originals that we just can't identify as such?

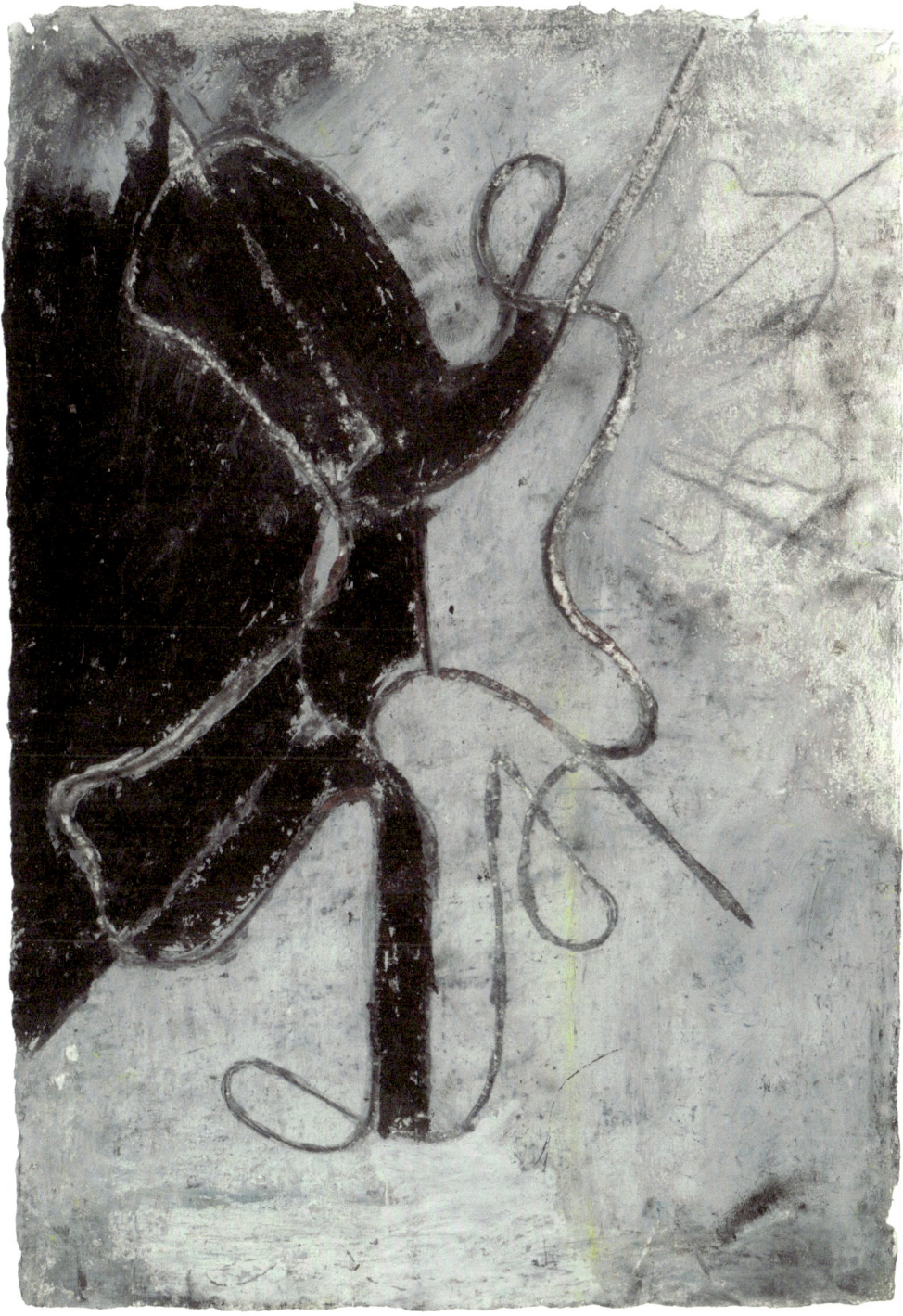

IV

There is a score to all
that isn't said a constant
buzz or hum enlarged
a pulse that soon becomes
like something sung or spoken
within there is a string
no, there are wavering

violins we bring
a tension like a wish
a wind along a wall
or laundry line and clothespins
marking time with keys
shifting through an un-
quaint calm and now
a chaos of tangled thinking's
twine, in a drawer,
a silent roar the world
is bound by secret knots,
they say, though what that means
is hard to know and flickers
so, also, and really
are those knots a noose
that hangs or ties that bind
our being stuck or held
together like a bridge
to build and cross or maybe
draw on or up
so no one can there is
a score to all that...

They seem like knots, or a strange music's notes on a staff, in a whorl, like petals opening, to be heard. Something scored. Scars or sores. A soaring. Drawing words.

It's the immediacy of ekphrasis that draws me. The contact. I realize it's odd to turn to another medium for a sense of immediacy. And yet, as with translation, that palpable sense of relation compels (completes?). And that's what I'm after – to speak into or through the drawings. To be dyed by their material qualities, as I feel them coming through me, or bringing me into their matrix. To take on their tinge.

Not transparency, but receptivity. Conduction.

As: another medium can sometimes be just that – a medium, through which a spirit's given voice (tenor, thickness, pitch).

'And this is poetry in the deepest sense – the art of being led and reaching that which goes beyond us.'
Odysseus Elytis

And, therefore, ekphrasis too implies a reaching leading to what's beyond. A conversation.

In its way a betweenness – that's all.

The darkness of a coupling, say; the recurring twist or torque of it. Because it's there on paper? Or in me – drawn out by the drawing? A little of each? I have no idea, really, but in this high-resolution Rorschach haze something collective is also tapped. At one drawing's center, doubled, floats the Hebrew letter *ayin*/ע – meaning an eye, or a natural fountain, a spring. Numerologically it stands for seventy, which in the tradition points to the number of nations, tongues, and 'faces' through which Scripture is steadily revealed. That is, it encodes the possibility of, and need for, ongoing interpretation (and stands for both translation and the impossibility...of rendering's ever coming to an end, which may be the truer meaning of the old saw that the work of translation is never done, since some translations are).

The materiality of the letter, of all letters – as building block and spirit trap, a grounding but insurgent tactility – lurks beneath our talk and verse, bringing us actually back to what matters, as matter, involving continual return to beginnings and incessant permutation. It offers us – in other words (and oddly with what words are made of) – a glimpse and deflected glint of the infinite. And so the letter leads to 'life', literally, here, to the faint Hebrew word חיים (*hayyim*), scribbled in the wings as well.
 Or not.
 L'hayyim.

A coupling's darkness.

V

Ink can twist it-
self around
and form a spring
from which things come
to figure infinity
in a glyph
or couple facing a pale
gray distance within
one
 another's ominous
shades further off and frailer
still but in the picture just
as well – like a trick
or quip – LIFE it seems
is pencilled in
a biblically cryptic script

VI

This writing's on and off the wall
and tells us what it is and why
we're so   intent on understanding
a layered saying that seems to say it
all and nothing in particular
just like everything seen by those
who know it shows at best the whole
in part that's growing with the telling
and spell   dangling   in between
like   someone listening into a
certain sort of uncertainty speaking
of uncertainty as a song
of songs truly tangled in our
being led along a luminous
line singed and limned within
the singing's seeing seeing us through

———

As someone else's vision disturbs – unsettles, alters, or interferes, perplexes, even hurts – ever so slightly with delight or anxiety, cadence or insight (through line and palette, perspective and timbre). To *describe* it, yes, 'portray in words', but also to 'form or trace by motion'.

VII

An ark so dark it
glows with its holding
the nothing it knows
within its unfolding

composing now
a hardening spark's
unhidden power
unbidden black

in diamond white
as softening graphite
crystal flaking
gently breaks

into an opaque
night of florescence
over a field
behind a fence

where a king's thinking
of slipping tenses
and the ancient art
of riding wakes

(or maybe only
a day's mistakes)
here at a pointed
end of a pencil

from a parcel
and that's a start
as ink shines
in the king's heart

Where the locus of value is: that ancient art of riding – a horse, a wave, a tiger, a hunch; two horses at once; around or into the ground, another sounding.

'It's a vale of tears out there', the dying writer said from his bed, and there's that score as well, the veil drawn or torn…

Meaning:

For all of the focus on materiality, there's something so much more-than-physical at stake in the movement between the drawing and the poem, through the rhythms of looking and listening, reading and reflection. 'Something grander than personality… the continuum, or "correlation"' – the critic quoting the quoting critic said – '"between life and matter."' That inflection. That infection. So that: the quality and nature of one's translations become the nature and quality of one's life?

He almost mistook a thin king for a queen's thinking and then he did, did and didn't, does still. The stakes are high… very high… he made a mystic?

A syllable soul-like thing, lost in non-translation, between registers of a day.

' 'Tis' he wrote at home in Concord, 'the use of life to learn metonymy', late in his...

And 'What, if not this deep translation, is your ardent aim?'
                    Rilke's Ninth Elegy

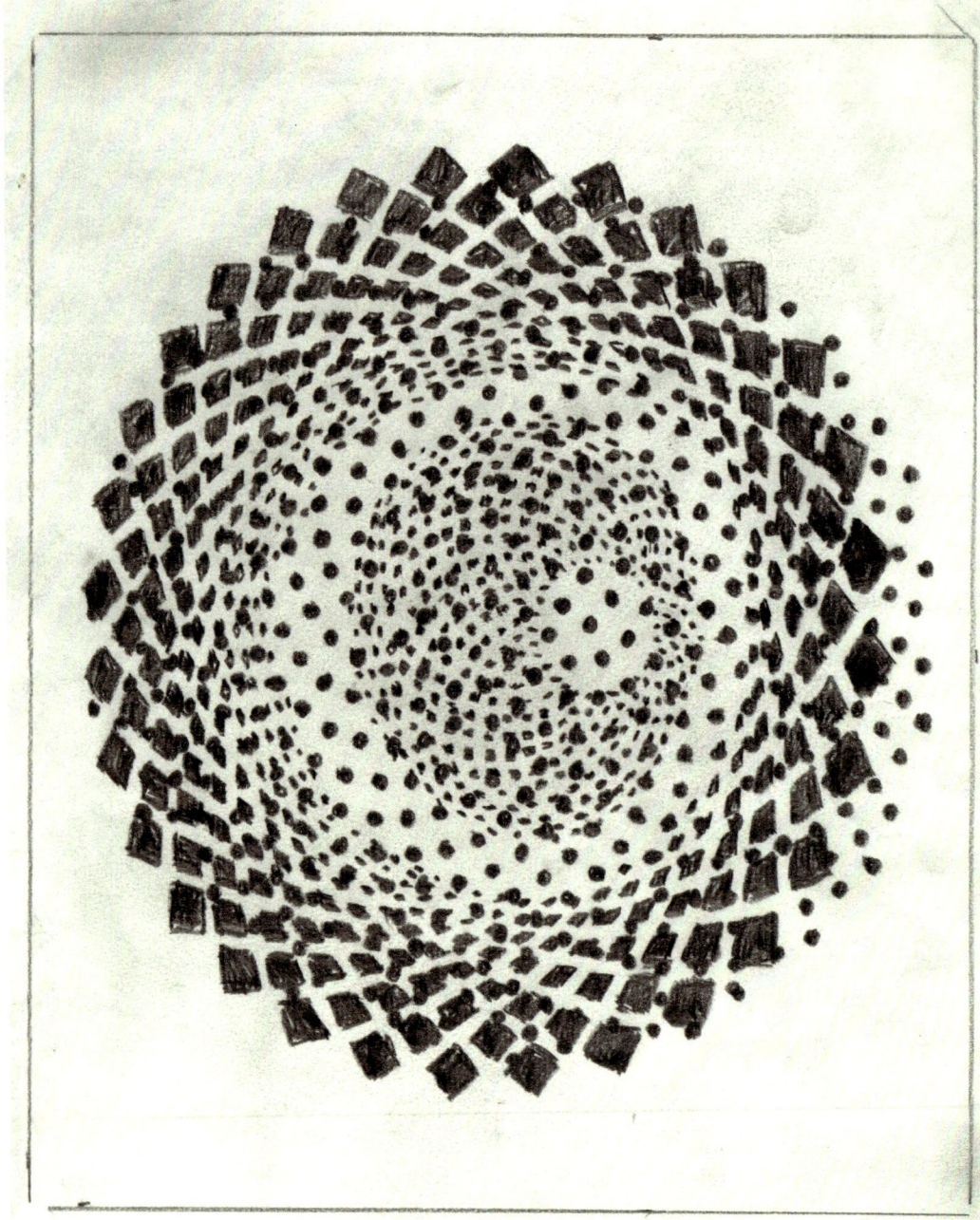

VIII

This world's dotty matrix calls
    and draws us toward a broken cause's
lozenged rose or window-wall
    and whorl or just a kind of clausal
contract-with-the-viewer you
    might be paying attention now
to the verb itself as somehow
    pay implies a currency in
a thicker economy of concentration
    and price that rhymes with sacrifice
which may be why these vortices bear
    spheres and diamonds in their whir
this morning's something we almost feel
    or feel but can't quite put into words
or give a name to   and that's the pearl
    a cone of dark that lets light through
a future via repetition's
    asking once and then again
a tension's moving around within
    what might be only a fancy screen
savored and caught in a nick of Time
    on a page we drift across
the day and toward its deckled edge
    giving way to what it suggests –
beauty's keeping secrets between us
    or screaming in silence to be seen
making a music of its emergency
    sail to a small magnificence or
this eddy's swirl's a pendant to
    a listening that's an end and means:
an eerie earring funneling care
    as hours that are always theres.

'You must sense', it's said the medium said, 'yourself as nothing
but an ear to hear the universe of the word

speaking through you'

as a present being drawn

through the sound that's passing on

IX

How *does* this drawer hold it
    all within a space
along a trace left
    on a surface marked
as such the world is drawn
    with water from a well
and then a gun or wagon,
    now a loan against
collateral, or interest on
    a bank account and maybe
a conclusion? Drapes
    are drawn so light gets in
or doesn't; someone draws
    attention drawing even
in a race he's drawn to,
    drawn aside or else
asunder, thus the luck
    of the draw we call it
has the drawing card
    drawing cheers, or blood,
a breath or blank or cello's
    bow, and so he drew
a bath or on a pipe
    as she drew fire and ducked,
the goose was shot and plucked
    then drawn as dawn drew near
they drew together playing
    on to a draw drawing
back and again to the
    drawing-board and plans
to hatch, or links to sketch
    like poems, yes, always
those to draw on there with-
    in the proverbial drawer.

Notes

5   *I guess the important thing:* Anne Carson, *Economy of the Unlost* (Princeton, 1990), p.viii.

13 *Draw me after:* from the pseudepigraphic foundational text of the Kabbalistic tradition, the thirteenth-century *Sefer ha-Zohar* (*Book of Radiance,* or *Splendor*). The citations here are from the *Zohar* to Song of Songs (*Zohar Hadash* 66c, 65c, and 65d, respectively).

13 *All the people saw the sounds:* Exodus 20:15. The translation is mine, and follows the exegetical Hebrew tradition.

15 *Levi Yitzhak of Berditchev:* A leading Hasidic figure in eighteenth-century central Poland, remembered for, among other things, his 'Dudele' (the 'Little Song of You'), which is quoted here. Peter Cole, *The Poetry of Kabbalah: Mystical Verse from the Jewish Tradition* (Yale, 2012), p. 236.

15 *My small skill to save:* John Berger, *Selected Essays*, edited by Geoff Dyer (Vintage, 2003), 'Drawn to that Moment', p. 420.

24 *And this is poetry in the deepest sense:* Odysseus Elytis, 'Nobel Address', translation mine.

32 *The critic quoting the quoting critic*: Christopher Lyon citing Richard Shiff, who is citing Gilles Deleuze, 'Oral History Interview with Terry Winters', November 13-15, 2018, Smithsonian Archives of American Art. https://www.aaa.si.edu/collections/interviews/oral-history-interview-terry-winters-17618.

33 *'Tis the use of life to learn:* Emerson, 'Poetry and Imagination', *Works of Ralph Waldo Emerson*, vol. 8, Letters and Social Aims, edited by Glen M. Johnson and Joel Myerson (Harvard, 2010/1875), p. 7.

33 *What, if not this deep translation:* The version cited is by William Gass, from his *Reading Rilke: Reflections on the Problems of Translation* (Dalkey Archive, reprint edition, 2015), p. 215.

36 *You must sense:* attributed to the eighteenth-century Hasidic leader Rabbi Dov Baer, known as the Maggid of Mezeritch. *Maggid* in Hebrew means 'story-teller' or 'preacher' (literally, 'sayer'); in Kabbalistic contexts it refers to an angel or celestial messenger who speaks through a receptive medium.

Picture Credits

All images by TERRY WINTERS
Images courtesy of the artist and Matthew Marks Gallery

FRONTISPIECE Detail of *Untitled*, 2016; graphite on paper, 11 × 8½ in.

7   *Untitled*, 2016; graphite on paper, 11 × 8½ in.
8   *Ennead/4*, 2012; graphite on paper, 9⅛ × 11½ in.
11 *Botanical Subject*, 1981; charcoal, chalk on paper, 29 × 19 in.
12 *Dark Plant 11*, 1982; crayon and charcoal on paper, 41½ × 29½ in.
14 *Untitled*, 1988; gouache and charcoal on paper, 30 × 22 in.
16 *"i"*, 1987; gouache on paper, 10¾ × 15 in.
17 *Schema (47)*, 1985–86; gouache and graphite on paper, 12 × 8½ in.
18 *Linking Graphics, 2*, 1999; ink, graphite, and coloured pencil on paper, 30½ × 44½ in.
21 *Schema (63)*, 1985–86; oil stick and graphite on paper, 12 × 8⅝ in.
22 *Untitled*, 2009; graphite and gouache on paper, 22 × 30 in.
26 *Schema (23)*, 1985–86; ink, graphite on paper, 12 × 8 ½ in.
28 *Animation*, 1996; charcoal, graphite, and oil on paper, 41⅝ × 29¾ in.
30 *Untitled*, 2009; graphite and ink on paper, 11 × 8½ in.
34 *Untitled*, 2011; graphite on paper, 11 × 8½ in.

ENDPIECE Detail of *Untitled*, 2016; graphite on paper, 11 x 8½ in.

COLOPHON

THE CAHIERS SERIES · NUMBER 36
ISBN: 978-1-909631-35-9

Series Editor: Dan Gunn
Associate Series Editor: Daniel Medin
Design: SYLPH EDITIONS DESIGN
Set in Giovanni Mardersteig's Monotype Dante

Text: © Peter Cole, 2020
Images: © Terry Winters, 2019
   Courtesy Matthew Marks Gallery

With thanks to the San Francisco Foundation for its generous support. Special thanks are also due to Claire Gilman and the Drawing Center (NY) for planting the seed of this cahier.

No part of this publication may be reproduced in any form whatsoever without the prior permission of the author or the publishers.

CENTER FOR WRITERS & TRANSLATORS
THE AMERICAN UNIVERSITY OF PARIS

SYLPH EDITIONS, LONDON | 2020

SYLPH
EDITIONS

www.sylpheditions.com · www.aup.edu

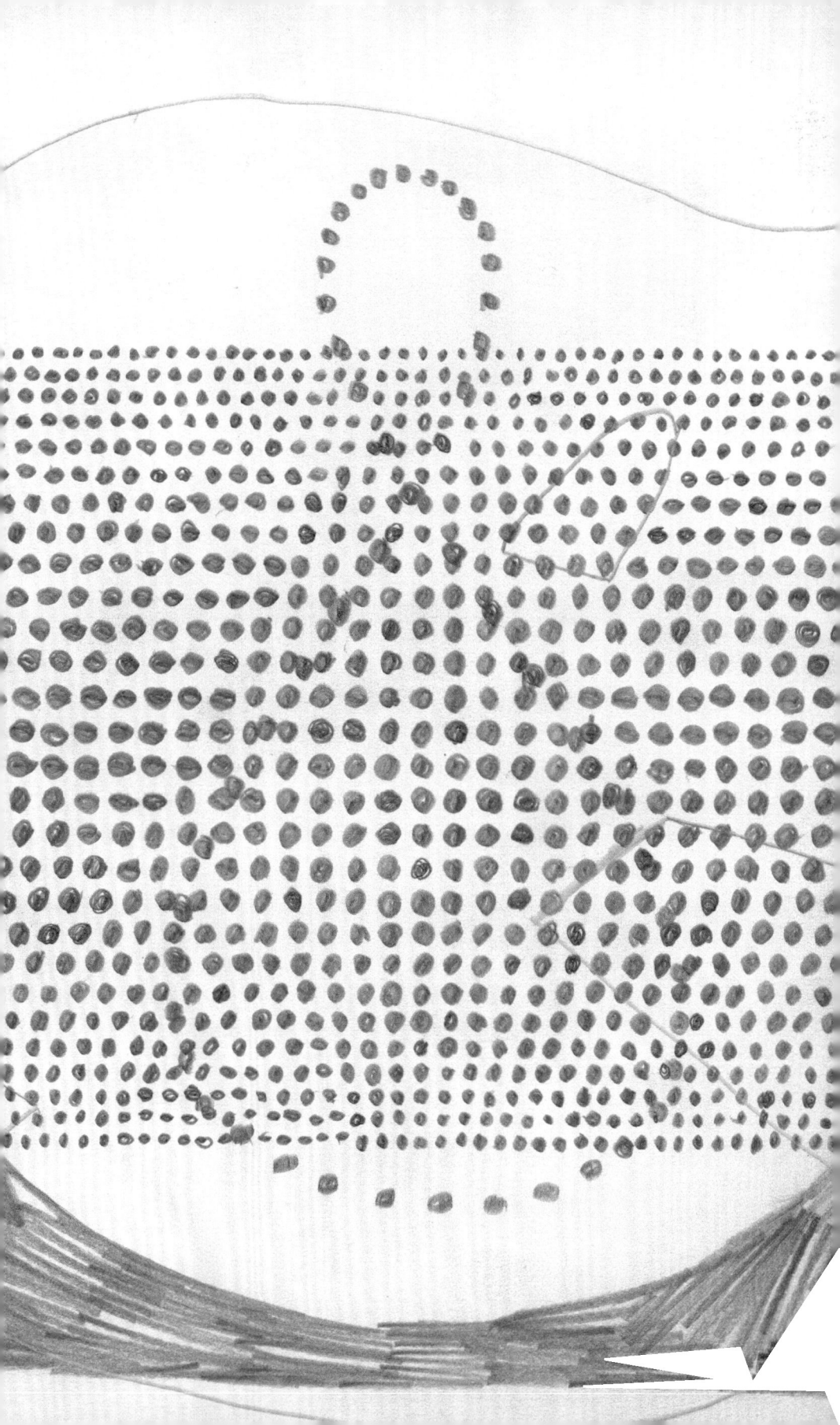